Copyright © 1974 by Platt & Munk, Publishers.
All rights reserved.
Printed in the United States of America.
Library of Congress Card Catalog No: 73-21344
ISBN: 0-8228-7701-5

Platt & Munk, Publishers/New York

SESAME STREET
BOOK OF OPPOSITES

with
ZERO MOSTEL

by
GEORGE MENDOZA

photography by SHELDON SECUNDA

book design by NICOLE SEKORA-MENDOZA

come

For Leslie McGuire and with special thanks to Allen Ducovny, Chris Cerf and Bernard Lang.

go

nice

grouchy

on

up

down

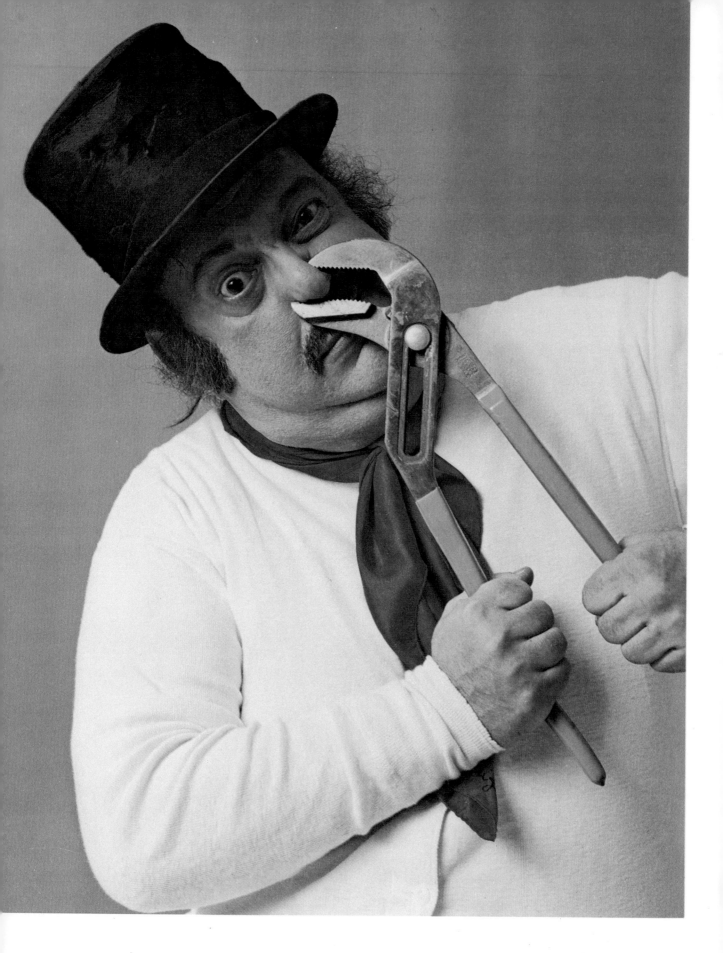

big

little

in

out

happy

sad

sit

stand

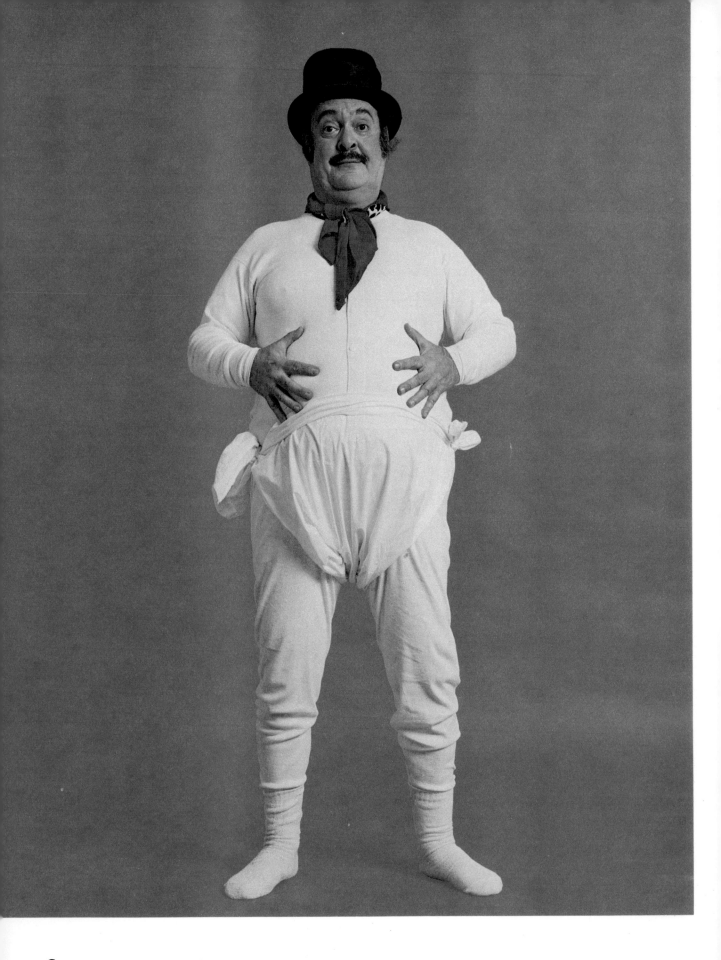

front

back

open

shut

yummy

yucchy

same

different

start

finish

short

tall

hello

goodbye

many

wet

dry

near

far

light

heavy

hot

cold

awake

asleep

When I first met Zero Mostel and asked him to do a book and film of opposites — a project I had conceived for Sesame Street — he looked at me with bulging Mostelian eyes and said:

"What are the children going to learn, what are opposites going to mean to children?"

I told Zero that teaching simple opposites like up and down, hot and cold, happy and sad helps build an understanding of basic relational concepts, and that I felt, as an experienced author of children's books, no one else in the world could match the hilarious human expressiveness of Zero Mostel.

Rehearsing the *Sesame Street Book of Opposites* with Zero Mostel was a fascinating, mind-in-flight experience. It would be difficult for me to forget that it took us nearly one hour to perfect on and off. But when I looked at Zero with his old black top hat leaning against the side of his face to illustrate off, I knew that no other image could replace the humor and impact of that sight.

I'm glad that Zero Mostel came back to be a teacher once more. And I know that children all over the world will be happy he did too.

George Mendoza